D1307647

THE
NETHERLANDS

Places and Peoples of the World

THE
NETHERLANDS

Steve Ozer

CHELSEA HOUSE PUBLISHERS
New York Philadelphia

COVER: Workers carry wheels of cheese through the cheese market, held every Friday
during the summer, at Alkmaar.

Chelsea House Publishers
Editor-in-Chief: Nancy Toff
Executive Editor: Remmel T. Nunn
Managing Editor: Karyn Gullen Browne
Copy Chief: Juliann Barbato
Picture Editor: Adrian G. Allen
Art Director: Maria Epes
Manufacturing Manager: Gerald Levine
Systems Manager: Rachel Vigier

Places and Peoples of the World
Editorial Director: Rebecca Stefoff

Staff for THE NETHERLANDS
Associate Editor: Ellen Scordato
Copy Editor: Karen Hammonds
Deputy Copy Chief: Mark Rifkin
Editorial Assistant: Marie Claire Cebrián
Picture Researcher: Patricia Burns
Assistant Art Director: Loraine Machlin
Designer: Donna Sinisgalli
Production Manager: Joseph Romano

First Printing
1 3 5 7 9 8 6 4 2

Library of Congress Cataloging-in-Publication Data
Ozer, Steve
The Netherlands
p. cm.—(Places and Peoples of the world)
Summary: Describes the history, geography, government, society,
economy, and culture of the Netherlands.
1. Netherlands—Juvenile literature. [1. Netherlands.]
I. Title. II. Series.
DJ18.093 1990   89-23842
949.2—dc20 CIP AC
ISBN 0-7910-1107-0

CONTENTS

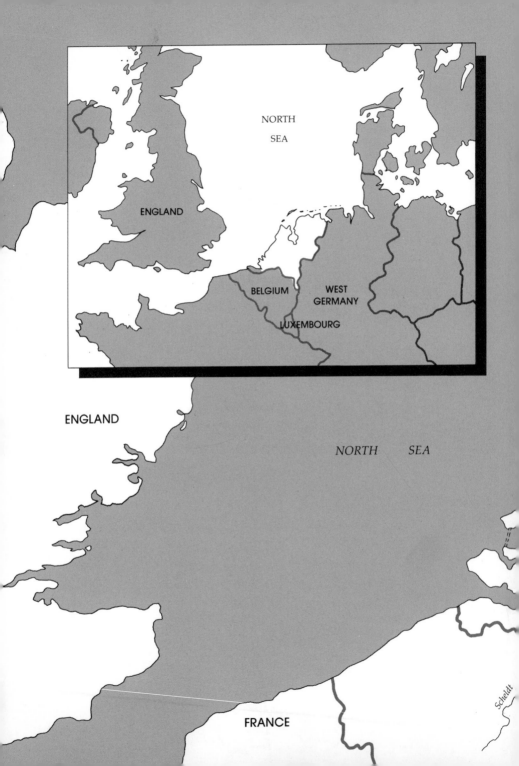

FACTS AT A GLANCE

Area	16,133 square miles (41,785 square kilometers)
Highest Point	The Vaalserberg, 1,053 feet (319 meters)
Greatest Length	190 miles (305.9 kilometers)
Greatest Width	120 miles (193.2 kilometers)
Major Rivers	Rhine, Maas, Scheldt
Population	14,615,000
Population Density	1,115.2 people per square mile (430.6 people per square kilometer)
Population Distribution	Urban, 88.4 percent; rural, 11.6 percent
Capital	Amsterdam
Seat of Government	The Hague
Major Cities	Amsterdam (population 679,140), Rotterdam (population 571,372), The Hague (population 443,961), Utrecht (population 229,933)
Languages	Dutch (official language), English, Frisian
Literacy rate	Virtually 100 percent

Ethnic Groups	Dutch, 96.2 percent; Turkish, 1 percent; Moroccan, 0.8 percent; German, 0.3 percent; other, 1.7 percent
Average Life Expectancy	Male, 73.1 years; female, 79.7 years
Official Religion	None
Religions	Roman Catholic, 36.2 percent; Dutch Reformed church, 18.1 percent; Reformed churches, 8.3 percent; no religion, 34.7 percent; other, 2.7 percent

Economy

Chief Exports	Refined oil, chemicals, iron and steel, dairy products, electronics, tulips
Chief Imports	Crude oil, iron ore, machinery
Chief Agricultural Products	Potatoes, sugar beets, lettuce, tomatoes, cucumbers, melons, pears, cherries, grapes, apples, and strawberries
Major Resources	Natural gas, salt, peat, gravel, sand, and clay
Industries	Chemicals, aircraft manufacture, shipbuilding, transportation equipment, electronics, fishing
Currency	Guilder, divided into 100 cents
Average Annual Income	Equal to U.S. $23,200

Government

Form of Government	Constitutional monarchy
Legislature	States-General, or parliament, divided into first and second chambers
Formal Head of State	King or queen
Head of Government	Prime minister
Local Government	Twelve provincial governments, or councils; local municipalities

HISTORY AT A GLANCE

2000 B.C. Stone Age tribes build huge piles of rocks, called Giants' Graves, as memorials to the dead.

500 B.C. The Frisians construct large islands of earth and clay, called terps, to stave off the North Sea.

58 B.C. The Romans conquer the Netherlands.

Early 400s A Germanic people called the Franks push out the Romans and lay claim to the Netherlands.

700 to 900 Vikings plunder and terrorize the coasts of northern and western Europe, including the Netherlands.

1200s Amsterdam, Rotterdam, and The Hague are built on new polders.

1300s to 1500s Dukes of Burgundy from France rule the Netherlands.

1516 The Burgundian duke Charles V, who inherited Burgundy and the Netherlands in 1506, becomes king of Spain.

1519 Charles V is named Holy Roman Emperor.

1556 Charles V abdicates and turns the reins of his empire over to his son, Philip II.

1568	Prince William of Orange launches attacks against King Philip II and the Spanish.
1579	Seven northern provinces declare their independence from Spain by signing the Union of Utrecht.
1584	Prince William of Orange is assassinated.
1600s	During the Golden Age, the Dutch build the largest shipping fleet in the world and produce brilliant artists, scientists, and thinkers.
1602	The Dutch government charters the Dutch East India Company.
1609	Henry Hudson explores a river in New York State, a bay in Canada, and a strait leading into the bay.
1626	The Dutch buy Manhattan Island for $24 from the American Indians. They claim colonies that are today the states of New York, New Jersey, Delaware, and Connecticut.
1648	The Eighty Years' War comes to an end when Spain recognizes the Netherlands' independence.
1700s	The Netherlands fights several wars with England and France for supremacy on the sea.
1815	King William I brings together the Netherlands, Belgium, and Luxembourg to form the Kingdom of the Netherlands.
1830	Belgium declares its independence.
1840 to 1849	William II oversees the transformation of government to a constitutional monarchy.
1849 to 1890	William III strengthens democracy in the Netherlands.
1890	Queen Wilhelmina succeeds William III.
1914 to 1918	The Dutch remain neutral during World War I.
1940	Germany invades the Netherlands in World War II. Rotterdam is bombed heavily.

1945	The Netherlands is liberated from German rule by the Allies.
1948	Queen Wilhelmina abdicates the throne and is succeeded by Queen Juliana.
1949	Indonesia is granted its independence from Dutch rule.
1953	A massive flood kills 1,800 people and destroys 50,000 homes.
1953 to 1986	The Dutch build the Delta Project to seal off the southwestern part of the country from the North Sea.
1980	Queen Juliana abdicates the throne and is succeeded by Queen Beatrix.
1989	The government unveils the most massive pollution cleanup program ever undertaken by any country.

The Netherlands and its people have been shaped by the sea. Large parts of the country were once covered by water, and only the industry and ingenuity of the Dutch reclaimed this land. The wealth of the nation has been mainly derived from shipping, and many Dutch—including this proud captain—enjoy leisure time on boats as well.

1

The Netherlands and the World

The nation of the Netherlands, sometimes called Holland after one of its most important provinces, lies in northern Europe on the shore of the North Sea. The stormy waters of this sea have threatened inhabitants of the region since recorded history began. Sixty percent of the population lives on land that is below sea level. In areas along the coast, the land dips as much as 22 feet (6.6 meters) below sea level. In few regions does the ground rise more than 330 feet (99 meters) above sea level. In fact, more than a quarter of all the land in the Netherlands is lower than the ocean itself, which is why the country was given its name; the Netherlands means "low lands."

How is it that the sea has not swallowed up this marshy patch of flat land? The answer lies with the Dutch, as the people of the Netherlands are called. For more than 4,000 years, the Dutch have fought to protect their land from the onrushing tide, from overflowing rivers, and from flooding lakes. They have devised clever ways to hold back the water and even reclaim land from the sea. The earliest people who lived in the area constructed great mounds of earth and clay called terps, on which they built their homes. They constructed entire villages on these man-made islands, which remained above water even at high tide.

In the thousands of years since then, the Dutch have devised increasingly sophisticated ways to deal with the encroaching sea. Today, hundreds of miles of huge walls, called dikes, line the ocean and rivers to keep out the water. Windmills, which at one time provided power to drain water from the land, have been replaced with electrically powered pumping stations. This complex system of dikes, dams, canals, and pumping stations prevents half of the Netherlands from being submerged. Through their resourcefulness and determination, the Dutch have turned lakes into farms, bogs into forests, and marshes into pastures. It is easy to see why the Dutch have a saying, "God made the world, but the Dutch made Holland."

The Netherlands is one of the world's smallest nations. However, it has influenced countries as large as the United States and as small as the Caribbean island of Curaçao. In the 1600s, known as the Golden Age of the Netherlands, this tiny nation built the biggest shipping fleet in the world. Dutch traders set sail for strange and exotic lands and returned with spices, tea, and silk. Dutch explorers traveled all over the earth. A Dutch sailor discovered a cape at the tip of South America and named it Cape Horn for his hometown, Hoorn, in the Netherlands. A group of Dutch farmers called Boers settled in South Africa. The Netherlands ruled over Indonesia and Ceylon, which lie between the South Pacific and Indian oceans, and over a group of islands in the Caribbean. In North America the Dutch settled in what today are the states of New York, New Jersey, Delaware, and Connecticut. In 1626, they bought a piece of land from American Indians for what today would be worth $24 and a few trinkets. Today, that land is New York City.

While the Dutch were claiming land around the world, back home their nation was home to some of the most talented people in history. Artists such as Rembrandt van Rijn, Jan Vermeer, and Frans Hals painted stunning portraits of wealthy merchants wearing rich velvet and silk clothing. Christian Huygens aimed his unique telescope toward the heavens and discovered the rings of Saturn. Antonie van Leeuwenhoek built the first microscope and gazed in awe at the millions of bacteria swimming in a drop of water. The Netherlands amazed the world with its talented artists, scientists, and thinkers.

Spotless electric pumping stations have replaced windmills as power sources in the Dutch system of water management. Such stations keep the sea from flowing back over drained areas of land called polders.

Impromptu performances are common in Amsterdam, especially in the summer when its narrow streets are crowded with young travelers. The city is a mecca for backpackers and students, who are drawn to its free-wheeling, creative atmosphere.

The Netherlands is no longer the great world power it once was. But it retains its preeminence in the area of international shipping. The harbor of Rotterdam is the busiest in the world. Rotterdam is located near the North Sea on the Nieuwe Maas River and is connected by canals to the Rhine River. These rivers are important paths of transportation for products coming into and out of Europe. Every year, 30,000 ships enter Rotterdam's harbors carrying products bound for France, Germany, Switzerland, and beyond. Products exported from Europe go through the city's ports on their way to countries throughout the world.

The rural regions of the Netherlands are noted for their peaceful charm. From the fertile soil grows the country's most well known crop—its beautiful tulips. In the spring, row after row of brightly colored crocuses, daffodils, and hyacinths create a magnificent patchwork of flowers. Millions of grazing cows dot the countryside. They provide the raw milk that goes into the cheese and other dairy products for which the Netherlands is well known.

The bucolic quiet of the Netherlands is in sharp contrast to its ongoing war with the sea. The Dutch will never forget a battle that occurred on January 31, 1953. On that night, the fiercest storm in memory whipped the North Sea into a frenzy. Winds howled up to 100 miles per hour. Huge waves rose up and crashed through the dikes. The results were tragic: 1,800 people lost their lives and 50,000 homes were covered with water.

The Dutch vowed never to experience another such tragedy. That year they began the Delta Project, one of the biggest public-works projects ever undertaken by a country. It took 33 years to complete. During that time, the Dutch built an intricate network of dikes and dams to seal off the southwestern part of the country from the sea. On October 4, 1986, Queen Beatrix officially opened the final storm-surge barrier. The massive Delta Project was complete.

The village of Pappendrecht in the province of South Holland was hard hit by the di-
sastrous flood of 1953. More than a quarter of the Netherlands lies below sea level, and
when a dike breaks, as this one did, the sea rushes in and covers the land.

2

The Low Lands

The Netherlands, located in northwestern Europe, is bounded to the north and west by the North Sea. To the east lies West Germany; to the south lies Belgium. Like the Netherlands, Belgium and its southeastern neighbor, Luxembourg, are flat and low-lying. Together, these three nations are known as the Low Countries.

At its longest point, the Netherlands measures just 190 miles (305.9 kilometers) from north to south. At its widest, it is 120 miles (193.2 kilometers) from east to west. Its area is 16,133 square miles (41,785 square kilometers), about one-half the size of the state of Maine. West Germany is 6 times bigger than the Netherlands, and France is nearly 14 times its size. Nearly one-sixth of the Netherlands is not land at all, but water. More than 2,500 square miles (6,500 square kilometers) of lakes, rivers, estuaries (the meetings of river mouths and ocean tides), and man-made canals cover the land.

To the west, the coastline along the North Sea is jagged and irregular. Stretches of water form inlets that bite deep into the land. Off the coast to the north lie the Frisian Islands. These islands are actually high-rising sand dunes, part of a strip that stretches along the coastline from north to south. The shifting sands of the islands and the channels of this area make it difficult and dangerous to navigate.

At one time an inland arm of the sea, called the Zuider Zee, carved out a nearly circular stretch of water on the north coast. However, in 1932 the Dutch finished construction of a barrier dam across the Zuider Zee that connects the provinces of North Holland and Friesland. This dam, which is 18.6 miles (30 kilometers) long and 100 yards (91 meters) wide, divides the ocean into the outer saltwater sea, called the Wadden Zee, and an inland freshwater lake, called the IJsselmeer.

The Low and High Netherlands

The Netherlands is divided into two major land regions—the Low and High Netherlands. The coastal provinces of Zeeland, South Holland, North Holland, Flevoland, Friesland, and Groningen form the Low Netherlands. The region is certainly well named. Nearly half of the Low Netherlands lies below sea level, and the other half rarely rises more than about three feet (one meter) above sea level. If not for the protection of the coastal dunes and dikes, the Low Netherlands would be completely underwater.

Land that has been diked off from the sea and drained of water is called a polder, or polderland. There are several hundred polders in the Low Netherlands, and all of them are kept habitable by steam, diesel, and electric pumps that work night and day to drain the land of excess water. A person standing in a polder can gaze at an unusual view. Because the land is below sea level, it is possible to look up at the surrounding dike and, beyond the dike, to catch a glimpse of the tops of sailboats and other vessels gliding by above.

The largest cities in the Netherlands, including Amsterdam, Rotterdam, The Hague, and Utrecht, are situated on polders. The bulk of the Dutch population is located in the western part of the country on a horseshoe-shaped area of polderland known as the Randstad. The dense population of the Randstad has spurred the government to maintain what the Dutch call the Green Heart. Strips of agricultural or recreational land separate the towns and cities. These refreshing changes in the landscape keep the concentrated populations of cities in the Randstad from spilling over into one another.

The low-lying lands in the southwestern part of the country have been particularly vulnerable to the whims of the North Sea. The disastrous flood of 1953 spurred the Dutch to design the Delta Project, and today the estuaries that jut into the land have been closed off with massive dams and dikes. One such arm of the sea, called the Eastern Scheldt, has been closed off by means of a massive storm-surge barrier. This barrier, nearly 2 miles (3.22 kilometers) long, is made up of 65 concrete piers and 62 steel gates. The gates normally remain up to allow the sea to flow in and out of the Eastern

The orderly, compact design of the town of Elburg in the Zuider Zee is typical of Dutch communities. Lines of trees on the perimeter act as windbreaks. In the background is the polder of East Flevoland.

The rural Dutch landscape is a peaceful one. Expanses of flat land are dotted with small country churches and farms below a sky full of billowing clouds.

Scheldt. But in stormy weather, the gates are lowered to protect the estuary from rising water levels that could lead to flooding.

The High Netherlands includes the provinces of Limburg, North Brabant, Utrecht, Gelderland, Overijssel, and Drenthe. *High* is a misleading term, however. Even in the High Netherlands, the ground rarely rises more than a few hundred feet above sea level. The highest point in the country is situated in the southeastern province of Limburg. A mountain called the Vaalserberg rises 1,053 feet (319 meters). The Vaalserberg would be considered merely a hill in nearby Switzerland, where the highest point towers at more than 15,000 feet (4,500 meters). In fact, the Vaalserberg is actually 200 feet (68 meters) shorter than the Empire State Building in New York City.

One of the most important rivers in Europe, the Rhine, winds through the Netherlands and empties into the North Sea. The Rhine begins in Switzerland, flows between France and Germany, and continues through Belgium before entering the Netherlands. Three smaller rivers in the Netherlands—the Waal, the Lek, and the IJssel—are branches of the Rhine. The Rhine, the Maas, and the Scheldt rivers serve as important means of transportation for products and materials coming into and out of Europe.

Climate and Weather

Inhabitants of the Netherlands enjoy a temperate climate—cool summers and mild winters. In July, the temperature averages about 63° Fahrenheit (17° Celsius). In January, the temperature averages about 35° F (2° C). The weather is a favorite topic of conversation among the Dutch. Although the average annual rainfall is a moderate 31 inches (790 millimeters), the rain is often unpredictable. Sometimes the sun will shine for weeks at a time. At other times the sunshine barely has time to peek through between the short rainsqualls. Some people never leave their homes without umbrellas.

The Netherlands is well known for its billowing clouds. Much of the wind sweeping over the country comes from the west, picking up moisture from the North Sea. This moisture in the air turns into clouds. On any given day, three-fifths of the sky is covered with piles of puffy clouds. For centuries, Dutch painters have rounded out their magnificent landscapes with depictions of the serene sky and its cotton-candy clouds.

Because much of the land is flat, there are few barriers to keep the wind from blowing across the country. Steady winds average 13 miles per hour (20.93 kilometers per hour) but diminish to less than half that in the hillier southern region. The Dutch have long been well aware of the power of the wind. In past centuries they made good use of its force by building windmills, but at the same time they recognized that it could scour away their valuable land. To keep the precious dunes from slowly blowing away, they have planted a type of dune grass called marram. The Dutch use brightly

Because the land is so flat, strong winds sweep easily across it. These beach goers have portable windscreens; sidewalk cafés often have glass-enclosed seating areas rather than outdoor tables to protect diners from the wind.

colored windscreens on the beach to protect against blowing sand. And even the sidewalk cafés use glass windscreens to keep the wind from playing havoc with customers' meals.

The natural vegetation in the Netherlands is dominated by dune grasses and other plants that can thrive in salt water. These rather plain grasses form a sharp contrast to the brilliant ornamental flowers planted by the Dutch. For good reason, the country has become known as the "florist for western Europe." In the fields that extend from the north of Leiden to the south of Haarlem, blazing fields of brightly colored tulips form a checkerboard against the horizon.

Trees are a precious commodity. Only about 8 percent of the land has trees, and most of the forests are located in the center of the country. The most common trees include birch, oak, and pine. Trees are so scarce that the government must grant permission for a landowner to cut down a tree in order to build a house. And for every tree that is cut down, another must be planted elsewhere on the property.

As the Dutch have drained water from new land and changed the face of nature, most of the animals native to the Netherlands have disappeared. The badger, river lobster, marsh turtle, and hawk are found no more. However, the North Sea still teems with an abundance of fish and shellfish that serve as an important food source for the Dutch. The herring is one of the most commercially important fish. Although the North Sea is still home to plenty of herring, the same cannot be said of the IJsselmeer. After the Zuider Zee was closed off in 1932, the inland lake became freshwater and lost its population of herring. Today, however, the herring in the IJsselmeer have been replaced with another favorite Dutch food: eels.

Oysters are also a popular Dutch delicacy. The government paid particular attention to these shellfish when designing the storm-surge barrier to close off the Eastern Scheldt. Instead of completely cutting off the ocean with a concrete barrier, engineers designed a system of gates that could open and close. That way, oysters would not be deprived of the tidal movement that they need to survive.

William the Silent, prince of Orange, led the Netherlands in the 1568 rebellion against Philip II of Spain. He is beloved by the Dutch as the founder of the Dutch Republic, although he was assassinated before the Netherlands was completely free of foreign domination.

3

Early History

Archaeologists have discovered crude stone weapons and tools in the Netherlands indicating that human beings inhabited the land 18,000 years ago. These early people did not settle in one place, however, but continually moved about in search of food and shelter. Evidence of the first settled tribes can still be seen along the eastern border with Germany, where these people heaped up huge piles of large rocks as memorials to the dead. These memorials, known as Giants' Graves, date back 4,000 years.

The most dramatic remnants of the past were made 2,500 years ago and can be seen today in the province of Friesland. There, tremendous mounds of earth and clay, called terps, stand out in stark silhouette against the cloudy sky. The Frisians, as the people in the northern region were called, built these islands in a valiant attempt to deal with the North Sea. They could construct an entire village on a terp, which served as a crude yet surprisingly effective way to survive in a hostile environment.

Other tribes, including Celtic people from central Europe and Germanic tribes from northern Europe, settled in the Netherlands. The Frisian, Celtic, and Germanic tribes looked different from one

*Piles of rocks called Giants'
Graves, built by some of
the earliest settled tribes in
what is now the Nether-
lands, can still be seen near
the West German border.*

another, and each had their own customs, dialects, and way of life. Today in the Netherlands, the various traditions in different provinces can be traced back to these earliest settlers.

In the 1st century B.C., the Netherlands was overrun by invading Romans, whose empire was expanding throughout Europe and the Mediterranean region. The people of the Low Countries were no match for the massive, well-organized army of Julius Caesar, and in 58 B.C., the Romans conquered the areas that are today the Netherlands, Belgium, and Luxembourg.

The conquest was a mixed blessing for the Dutch. Although the people no longer had their independence, the Roman invaders taught them how to build highways, towns, and more effective dikes. All was not peaceful under Roman rule, however, and the Dutch rose up in revolt from time to time. These uprisings were unsuccessful until the Roman Empire began to crumble in the 4th century A.D. A Germanic people called the Franks pushed out the Romans in the early 5th century A.D. and laid claim to a kingdom that included the present-day countries of the Netherlands, Belgium, France, and part of Germany.

The Franks did not rule over all of the Netherlands. The tough and determined Frisians refused to accept the rule of the invading Frankish tribes. Even though Clovis, king of the Franks, converted to Christianity in 496 and demanded that the Dutch accept the new religion, the Frisians continued to pray to pagan gods for another 200 years. Only the Frankish emperor Charlemagne's threat of armed enforcement in the 8th century finally compelled the Frisians to adopt Christianity.

After the death of Charlemagne in A.D. 814, the Frankish kingdom weakened. Thirty years later, it was divided among Charlemagne's grandsons. Charles ruled in what is today France. Louis reigned over what is roughly Germany now. And a third grandson, Lothair, ruled over the rest of the Frankish kingdom, including the Netherlands.

Well equipped and highly disciplined, the Roman army under Julius Caesar swept through most of western Europe in the 1st century B.C. This carving depicts a Roman troop ship. The area that is now the Netherlands fell before this onslaught in 58 B.C.

The Dutch faced daunting troubles at that point. Not only had they lost their independence, but they continued to struggle against the sea. To make matters worse, they faced a new threat: Vikings. Vikings were Scandinavian seafarers who plundered and terrorized the coasts of northern and western Europe from the 8th to the 10th centuries A.D. For 200 years, the Dutch were subject to vicious, unpredictable raids by these fierce Norwegians and Danes. Without warning, Vikings would wreak havoc an unsuspecting villages—robbing, enslaving, and even murdering terrified villagers. And just as quickly, the Vikings would disappear.

The Dutch villagers, desperate for protection, turned to rich noblemen who had built fortresslike castles on huge tracts of land throughout the Netherlands. Seeking refuge, some of the people built houses on the noblemen's land. There, in return for protection,

Vikings from the Scandinavian peninsula sailed the North Sea from A.D. 700 to 900. Coastal settlements in the Low Countries were defenseless against these ferocious warriors, who terrorized villagers with swift raids from the sea.

they performed services, raised crops, and sometimes paid rent and taxes to the noblemen. This social system was called feudalism, and versions of it flourished throughout Europe during the later Middle Ages (usually considered to be the period between 900 and 1500).

In the 1100s and 1200s, the size of the Netherlands grew, as new polders were claimed from the sea. The people diked off and drained lakes and swamps along the coast, creating new land on which to build houses and farms. In the 1200s, the cities of Amsterdam, Rotterdam, and The Hague were built on these new polders.

The Dutch continued to be ruled by outsiders in the years that followed. From the 1300s to the 1500s, the Netherlands, along with what would become Luxembourg and Belgium, was ruled by the dukes of Burgundy from France. This period was known as the Burgundian Dynasty. One of the most significant developments in European history occurred toward the end of this period.

In the first decades of the 1500s, a German priest and theologian named Martin Luther began to criticize the Roman Catholic church. His teachings led to a split in Christianity and the growth of Protestantism. Lutheranism (based on Luther's teachings) and Calvinism (based on the teachings of the Swiss theologian John Calvin) became the two main branches of Protestantism. Calvinism attracted many believers in the northern part of the Low Countries, where the Netherlands is located. Inhabitants of the regions that are now Belgium and Luxembourg remained mostly Roman Catholic.

One of the dukes of Burgundy, Charles V, ruled over the Netherlands as well as a vast empire of European countries; in 1516, he inherited the kingdom of Spain. Although the Dutch thus came under Spanish rule, Charles V was seen as a decent and fair ruler, one whose wisdom and moderation eased religious tensions between Catholics and Protestants.

At the end of 1556, Charles gathered all of his delegates from the Low Countries together in Belgium for what would be an emotional speech. In frail health, Charles leaned on the shoulders of a young man named William, prince of Orange, as he addressed the crowd. Tears began to flow in the audience as Charles told his hearers that it was time to turn the reins of his empire over to his son, Philip II. He asked that they show the same allegiance and devotion to Philip as they had to Charles himself during his 40 years of rule. Then he introduced Philip.

The tears stopped as soon as Philip began to speak. He spoke in Spanish, instead of Dutch or French, and the rigidity of his plans for the future was in great contrast to the warmth and compassion of his father.

In the succeeding years, the Dutch would learn just how different Philip was from his father. Unlike Charles, who was known for promoting religious tolerance, Philip was determined to convert his entire empire to Catholicism. Although Belgium and Luxembourg had long been Catholic, many in the Netherlands had firmly embraced Calvinism, known for its values of orderliness and austerity. Philip resorted to intimidation and violence to limit religious freedom. He installed a military force in the Low Countries, ordered Protestants put to death, and stripped away the rights of those who would not agree with him.

The Dutch were pushed to the brink. Having suffered through more than 1,500 years of foreign domination, they were determined to resist religious persecution by a Spanish king. But they needed a leader. They needed someone with the courage and vision to lead a revolt against what looked like insurmountable odds. The Dutch turned to the man on whom King Charles had leaned during his emotional farewell speech: William, prince of Orange.

The son of a rich count, William had inherited a great amount of land in the Netherlands, as well as the principality of Orange in France. At an early age, William had become a favorite member of the court of King Philip. He was admired for being a good listener,

Philip II became king of Spain and ruler of the Netherlands, which was then ruled by the duke of Burgundy, upon the abdication of his father. Philip's religious intolerance and attempts to keep his people Catholic sparked the Netherlands' long-fought but successful battle for independence.

one who would keep his ears open and speak only after careful thought. Thus, he became known as William the Silent.

At the age of 11, William had become a Roman Catholic as a condition of receiving his vast inheritance. But in later years, he became more and more interested in Calvinist teachings. Although he served in the court of a Roman Catholic king, William had secretly come to profess Calvinist beliefs. And he was more and more disturbed by the religious persecution that was taking place under King Philip, filling the land with violence and dividing its people. Finally William could take no more.

In 1566, William openly proclaimed his Calvinist faith and left the Netherlands for Germany. His goal was to build an army and

An engraving depicts scenes of jubilation in Leiden when the city's starving population received supplies of food at last after heroically resisting a months-long siege by Spanish forces.

return to rescue his homeland. The revolution began in 1568, when William launched a series of attacks against King Philip II and the Spanish.

At first, William and his army were more successful fighting battles on the sea than on land. In 1573, the Spanish suffered a humiliating defeat when their ships became stuck in ice in the Zuider Zee, an inland arm of the North Sea. The weather had turned suddenly cold, stranding the vessels in ever-thickening blocks of ice. The Dutch waited until the ice was solid enough, then stormed across the frozen sea on horseback to capture the Spanish.

That same year, an important event occurred that provided both a military and a psychological boost to the Dutch. The Spanish had surrounded the city of Leiden. For months, the citizens of Leiden resisted the onslaught, even though thousands died from hunger and disease. In 1574, acting on an order from William of Orange, the dikes were cut, unleashing a furious rush of water that finally drove out the Spanish.

William was deeply moved by the courage and tenacity of the people of Leiden. As a token of his appreciation, he offered the citizens a choice. He would either free them from taxation or establish a university in their city. Realizing that a relief from taxes might only be temporary, they chose the latter, and in 1575, the University of Leiden opened its doors. More than 400 years later, it remains the leading institution of higher learning in all of the Netherlands.

On January 23, 1579, the seven northern provinces of the Netherlands and several small cities in the south signed the Union of Utrecht. The Union of Utrecht called for an indivisible union in which each province could determine its own religion and in which no persecution would be tolerated. Two years later, the Dutch declared their independence, and William of Orange was named head of the government and army.

He would not live to see his country set free. On July 10, 1584, William was killed by an assassin. But the popular support for his mission did not die with him. The revolution that had begun in 1568 became known as the Eighty Years' War because it was not until 1648 that Spain recognized the Netherlands' independence. William of Orange went down in history as the Father of the Netherlands. To this day, his name has been immortalized in the Dutch national anthem, "Wilhelmus van Nassouwe," and his memory is enshrined in the hearts and minds of the people of the Netherlands.

Journael ofte gedenckwaerdige Befchrijvinge,
Van de acht-Jarige / ende feer Avontuerlijcke
R E Y S E, *Van*

WILLEM YSBRANTSZ.
BONTEKOE van HOORN,
Gedaen nae

OOST-INDIEN;
Begrijpende veel wonderlijcke ende gevaerlijcke faecken,
hem op defelve R E Y S E weder-varen.

Oock is hier by gevoeght een V E R H A E L, van
D I R C K   A L B E R T S Z.   R A V E N,
Commandeur op 't Schip Spitsbergen, gedeftineert na Groenlandt.

UTRECHT, By J U R I A E N van P O O L S U M, Ordinaris Stadts Drucker,
wonende op de Plaets / recht tegen over 't Stadhuys. ANNO 1684.

*The Dutch were intensely curious about the new lands visited by explorers in the 1600s.
This book, published in Utrecht, details one of the early journeys to the East Indies and
describes another that ended in a disastrous shipwreck.*

4

The Golden Age and Recent History

The 1600s were known as the Golden Age of the Netherlands. For more than 100 years, this tiny nation in northwestern Europe dominated the world both economically and culturally.

The Golden Age was bankrolled by the economic expansion in the Netherlands during the first half of the 17th century. By 1625, the Dutch had built the largest shipping business in the world. Hundreds of Dutch ships set sail for distant and exotic lands and returned with valuable goods. Traders returned from Mediterranean countries bearing luxurious silk and fine wines. They brought wool from England, delicate porcelain from China, and cinnamon, pepper, and cloves from the Moluccas (Indonesian islands in the South Pacific Ocean).

The Dutch traded with countries in Europe, Africa, and Asia and with settlements in America. But it was the lure of riches from the area bordering the Indian Ocean that inspired the greatest number of seafarers. Many individual companies had undertaken the difficult and often perilous voyages to Ceylon, mainland India, and Indonesia (the area then called the East Indies). In 1602, the

Netherlands' government acted to reduce the costs and to increase the security of these companies by chartering the Dutch East India Company, which spread the risks and costs of the various journeys among a number of companies. The Dutch East India Company became a powerful trading enterprise, one of the world's first joint-stock companies, enriching the coffers of its shareholders. When the ships returned after a year-long voyage to the East Indies, shareholders reaped profits as much as 50 percent above their original investment. The riches were staggering.

Exploration and Discovery

The lure of trade was not the only reason the Dutch set sail during the Golden Age. Curiosity and a love of adventure played a big role. Dutch explorers traveled the globe in search of undiscovered lands on which to raise the flag of the Netherlands. In 1596, Cornelis de Houtman landed three ships on the island of Java, claimed it for the Netherlands, and returned home two years later to the sound of church bells and the cheers of crowds in Amsterdam.

In 1609, the Dutch East India Company hired an English explorer named Henry Hudson to sail northwest and search out a passage to China and the Moluccas by way of the Atlantic Ocean. Hudson's curiosity got the best of him, however. He veered off his original course and explored the eastern seaboard of North America. Several of the waterways he sailed were named after him, including a river in what became New York State (the Hudson River), a bay in Canada (Hudson Bay), and a strait leading into that bay (Hudson Strait).

A few Dutch explorers reached Australia, but the Dutch did not have much interest in the continent. Dutch explorer Abel Tasman discovered an island in the South Pacific and named it New Zealand, after the province of Zeeland in the Netherlands. He was also the first European to explore an island off the southern coast of

Australia. Today that island is called Tasmania, and the adjacent body of water is called the Tasman Sea.

The Dutch controlled many of these distant lands under a political system called colonialism. These newly settled lands became colonies of the Netherlands, governed by Dutch officials and dependent upon the mother country for many of their economic needs. The Dutch claimed what are today the states of New York, New Jersey, Delaware, and Connecticut and named them New Netherland. They built a town named New Amsterdam on land they bought in 1626 for a pittance from the American Indians. It was later renamed New York City.

The Dutch staked claims in many other parts of the world. They settled part of Brazil in South America. They seized a group of islands in the Caribbean and named them the Netherlands Antilles. They eventually traded what is today New York State for a country called Suriname in South America. A group of Dutch farmers called

Workers on Banda Island in the Moluccas, in Indonesia, prepare nutmeg for export. The fortunes of the Golden Age were built on cargoes of spices from Indonesia. Spices were highly valued in the 1600s, for they not only flavored food but also preserved it in the era before modern refrigeration and canning.

Antonie van Leeuwenhoek, a Dutch scientist, was the first to explore the microscopic world, gazing through lenses he ground himself. His revolutionary descriptions of blood cells and bacteria astonished his contemporaries and paved the way for the discoveries upon which modern medicine is based.

Boers settled in South Africa. The Netherlands was at the height of its colonial powers in the 17th century, when its red, white, and blue flag flew over lands on almost every continent.

Flowering of Arts and Culture

While the Dutch were settling lands throughout the world, at home they were experiencing a magnificent flowering of arts and culture. The immense fortune that poured into the Netherlands paid for much more than the basic necessities of living. Wealthy merchants and traders adorned their homes with stunning, richly detailed paintings of themselves and their families. They commissioned painters to capture their likenesses on canvas, replete in their opulent silk, velvet, and fine embroidered fabrics.

The Golden Age produced a profusion of great painters, including Rembrandt, Frans Hals, Jan Vermeer, Pieter de Hooch, and Jacob van Ruisdael. Dutch painters did much more than simply paint portraits of the rich; they also captured the flavor of everyday life in the Netherlands. Simple people doing ordinary things became favorite subjects of Dutch painters in the 17th century. The proud baker in a painting by Jan Steen displays his loaves of fresh bread. A sad and thoughtful kitchen maid pours milk from a jug in a painting by Jan Vermeer. Skaters glide across the ice as beggars ask for alms in a painting by Hendrik Avercamp.

The Golden Age was also a time of great scientific and philosophical achievement in the Netherlands. Christian Huygens (1629–95) perfected a telescope and was the first to discover the rings of Saturn. His scientific curiosity led him to explore new ideas about gravity, and he invented a type of pendulum clock that is still found in living rooms throughout the Netherlands.

Like Huygens, Antonie van Leeuwenhoek (1632–1723) was fascinated with optics. However, instead of pointing a telescope toward the stars, he invented a simple microscope and focused the lenses on closer objects. He peered at a drop of water and was awed by the thousands of "wee animals"—bacteria and protozoa—swimming about. Amazed by this new unseen world, Leeuwenhoek focused his microscope on insects, drops of blood, human hairs, pieces of skin, and other common and uncommon items.

During the 1700s, the Netherlands became embroiled in several wars, mostly involving England and France, as these nations fought for supremacy on the sea. Gradually, the Netherlands declined in importance as the economic and colonial power of England and France grew. After the French Revolution, French forces invaded the Low Countries in 1795, and the Dutch political structure collapsed.

The Batavian Republic was established by French revolutionaries in 1795 and lasted until 1806, when the French emperor Napoleon created what he called the Kingdom of Holland and made his brother Louis its king. Upon Napoleon's defeat at Leipzig in 1813, the Dutch regained control of their nation. In 1815, William I, a descendent of the original prince of Orange, brought together the Netherlands, Belgium, and Luxembourg to form the Kingdom of the Netherlands. In 1830, Belgium declared its independence, and Luxembourg was divided between the Netherlands and Belgium.

William I, dismayed by the loss of Belgium, turned over the throne to his son William II in 1840. Although he was not perceived as a strong leader, William II brought about a transformation in government that remains in place today. Under his reign, a new constitution was written, modeled after that of England. The constitution called for the legislative duties of government to be placed in the hands of an elected body: the States-General. The monarch would act as the head of state. This type of government is called a constitutional monarchy.

William II died in 1849 and was succeeded by his son, William III, who carried on the ambitious transformation of government begun by his father. During his more than 40 years of rule, William III strengthened democracy in the Netherlands and started to share political power with a greater portion of the population by allowing more people to vote.

Between the early 19th century and World War I (1914–18), the Netherlands' economy was transformed. The role of agriculture diminished as that of industry grew. The textile, chemical, and early electrical industries, among others, took root in the Netherlands and helped to modernize the country. Rotterdam became one of the busiest ports in the world, and the Dutch people enjoyed increasing prosperity.

In 1890, King William III was succeeded by Queen Wilhelmina, who was crowned at the age of 10. Because of her young age, her mother ruled for 8 years until Wilhelmina was 18. There were many political squabbles during the early part of her reign, as religious political parties argued for their own state-supported schools and other parties sought voting rights for more of the population. On the eve of World War I, both sides reached an agreement. As conservatives wished, religious schools would receive funds from the state, and to satisfy the liberals in exchange, all adult males in the Netherlands would be granted the right to vote.

Putting this agreement, called the Pacification, into action had to be postponed when a greater concern united the Dutch: World War I. Although the Netherlands remained neutral during the war, the Dutch had to struggle to maintain their economy because the war severely reduced international trading as enemy nations blockaded each other's ships. The Pacification was put into effect when the war ended, bringing total equality to public and parochial schools and creating a more democratic government.

World War II

The Dutch could not choose to remain neutral in World War II. On May 10, 1940, Nazi Germany invaded the Netherlands. Within one week, the Nazis controlled the country. On May 13, Queen Wilhelmina and government officials fled to England, where they promptly set up a government-in-exile. The next day, the city of Rotterdam was gutted by bombs.

The Nazis demonstrated a particular hatred for the Jews, and began to systematically deport the Dutch Jews to concentration camps in Germany, where most were murdered or died of disease and starvation.

Anne Frank was one of the Jews persecuted by the Germans. Frank was the daughter of a Jewish businessman, Otto Frank. Otto moved his family to Amsterdam from Germany during the early part of the Nazi regime. But it was to no avail. On July 9, 1942, faced with deportation to a concentration camp, Otto went into hiding with his wife, two daughters, and four other people.

They hid in the back office and warehouse of his food business and were able to survive through the help of non-Jewish friends who brought them food and supplies. For more than two years,

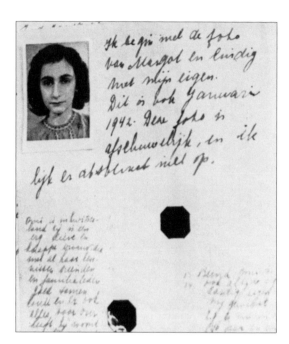

Anne Frank and her family hid for two years from the Nazis. Her tragic story has become familiar to millions of readers the world over through her diary, a moving testament to the suffering caused by the Holocaust and the resilience of the human spirit.

Anne Frank and her family lived in fear: To be discovered would mean certain death. During this time, Anne kept a meticulous diary that chronicled the pain and sorrow, the brief moments of joy, and the trials of growing into adolescence under these adverse conditions.

On August 4, 1944, the Germans acted on a tip from one of a few Dutch who collaborated with the Nazis and raided the Franks' hiding place. The family's worst fears came true. The Franks were shipped to Auschwitz, a concentration camp in Poland. Anne's mother died there in 1945. Anne and her sister were shipped to another camp, where they died of typhus. Otto Frank was rescued when the Russians liberated Auschwitz in 1945. Anne Frank's diary was published in 1947, and for generations it has captivated readers who have come to see the pain of World War II through that of a single victim.

The whole country suffered terribly throughout the war. Its cities were severely damaged by bombings, and starvation afflicted much of the population. The Netherlands was finally freed when Germany was defeated in 1945, and the Dutch prepared to rebuild. And just as the Dutch had yearned to govern their own nation once again, so did the colonies that had been under Dutch rule since the 17th century. Indonesia, which was occupied by Japan during World War II but which returned to Dutch rule after the war, struggled for independence. After a long, bloody revolution swept the country, the Netherlands granted independence to Indonesia in 1949. The island colony called the Netherlands Antilles in the Caribbean remained a part of the Kingdom of the Netherlands but was allowed to govern itself. Suriname in South America became independent in 1975.

Wilhelmina abdicated the throne in 1948 and was succeeded by her daughter Juliana. Just five years later came one of the Netherlands' greatest tragedies. The flood of 1953 took 1,800 lives and stunned the nation. That year, the government began construction of the Delta Project to seal off the southwestern part of the country from the unpredictable North Sea. Queen Beatrix succeeded Queen Juliana in 1980 and six years later dedicated the final storm-surge barrier of the Delta Project. Finally, the Dutch had fought off their worst enemy: the sea.

A woman appraises eels, a favorite Dutch delicacy, on sale at an outdoor market in Amsterdam. The Dutch diet relies heavily on seafood.

5

The Dutch Way of Life

The Dutch personality has been shaped in great part by religion and by the struggle with nature. Calvinism has ingrained a sense of austerity in the people; the constant battle against the encroaching sea has imparted a sense of practicality. The Dutch do not take to fancy cars and clothes or to flamboyant life-styles. Many prefer the simple pleasures of home and hearth. A typical Dutch woman may pass up an expensive piece of jewelry and instead buy something to make her family's home more comfortable.

There is an old Dutch saying, "Your own hearth is worth gold." Indeed, on a typical night in the Netherlands, many families sit comfortably in their living rooms, sharing the ups and downs of the day, reading their evening newspapers, or quietly watching television. The Dutch are a home-loving people. Their language includes a word that describes a feeling of coziness, comfort, and pleasure: *gezellig*. A gezellig evening might be spent at home with friends, having a quiet, informal dinner. It could be a low-key celebration of a family member's birthday. Or it could simply be a night devoted to practicing the violin.

For the Dutch, comfort and cleanliness go hand in hand. The people of the Netherlands have an international reputation for keeping spotless homes. They take great pride in keeping living areas *netjes*, or clean and tidy. Windows are always polished to a high sheen. Homemakers scrub floors, dust furniture, sweep sidewalks, clean woodwork, and straighten rooms. This passion for cleanliness climaxes in the *grote schoonmaak*, or spring cleaning. For two to three weeks every spring, the house is turned upside down to get at every last bit of dust and dirt missed during the daily cleaning ritual.

At one time, the Dutch had a unique style of dress. The men wore baggy pants and colorful round hats with wide brims. The women wore long, flowing dresses and lace bonnets or caps. Today, most people dress in modern clothes. However, a few people in Zeeland and the West Frisian Islands still wear traditional clothing. During many holidays, some Dutch dress up in the distinctive clothing of the past.

Around the world, the thought of the Dutch brings to mind wooden shoes. Wooden shoes, or *klompen*, have been a part of Dutch life for hundreds of years. Klompen help to keep the feet dry and warm in the rain and are worn by people who work outdoors, such as fishermen, farmers, and gardeners.

The Dutch preference for the simple and unadorned is obvious in their meals. Compared to the rich foods of the French or the elaborate meals of the Italians, the plain, wholesome food of the Netherlands serves more to nourish than to impress. Breakfast usually begins with a steaming cup of tea, followed by a boiled egg, a few slices of Dutch cheese, a basket of rolls and bread, and sausage or other meats. Coffee at midmorning, called *kopje koffie*, is not to be missed.

Lunch might be a spread of cold cuts, breads, cheese, and a salad. Dinner is the main meal of the day. It might begin with a thick pea soup, called *erwtensoep*, or with a clear broth, called *groentensoep*, filled with miniature meatballs, vegetables, and noodles. One traditional favorite meal is called *hutspot*, a hodgepodge of potatoes, carrots, and onions. Seafood is plentiful and popular in the Netherlands and is a mainstay at the dinner table. Green herring, those caught during the first three weeks of the fishing season in May, are a delicacy. Dutch shrimps, sole, oysters, and eels are a few other Dutch favorites.

A Sense of Order

The country's ongoing struggle with the sea is said to account for the sense of order that pervades Dutch society. For thousands of years, people have had to work together organizing, planning, and preparing to fight back the rising tides. This sense of organization has spilled over into everyday life. Almost everything needed to

Three elderly Dutch people walk to a festival sporting the traditional dress of their area. Such sights are increasingly rare in the modern Netherlands, as a curious passerby's look demonstrates.

run a household is efficiently delivered to the door—not only newspapers and milk but also meats, vegetables, breads, fruit, and soap. Many buildings are equipped with pulley systems to lift up the deliveries for those who live above the first floor.

Planning and organization have served the country well, as the Dutch have had to squeeze a population of 14,615,000 people into only 16,133 square miles (41,785 square kilometers). In 1965, the Netherlands enacted the Physical Planning Act. This legislation brought together the duties and powers of the central, provincial, and local governments to organize land efficiently for housing, recreation, trade, industry, agriculture, and transportation. But even before this act, the government made provisions to ease the housing burden on the population. After World War II, the government offered grants to individuals to build new homes or to improve existing ones. Today, the government provides grants to people whose income cannot sufficiently cover rents and other living expenses. The government gives special consideration to the elderly, the disabled, and even the single or two-person household.

The Dutch way of life is organized along religious lines. Nearly every aspect of living—schools, hospitals, newspapers, television stations, and even stores—is clearly either Catholic or Protestant. About 36 percent of the population are Roman Catholic; nearly 20 percent are Dutch Reformed (Protestant). Although people of different religions intermingle much more today than in times past, it is still common for a Dutch Catholic to attend a Catholic school, go to a Catholic dance, read a Catholic magazine, stay in a Catholic hospital, and marry in a Catholic church.

The Dutch pursue a variety of occupations. The country has a great concentration of government workers; 15 percent of its people work for either the national, provincial, or local governments, on a government committee, or are hired to research an ongoing problem. The Hague, where the seat of government lies, teems with government workers in dark suits and white shirts.

Manufacturing, however, accounts for the greatest number of workers in the Netherlands. About one in every three people works in the manufacture of iron and steel, chemicals, dairy products, ships, aircraft, electronics, clothing, or other industries. More than 800,000 people work in agriculture, cultivating the land to produce fruits and vegetables, or in raising livestock. Only a few thousand people today make their living through fishing. The rest of the population are engineers, biologists, doctors, lawyers, shopkeepers, bus drivers, and others who work in just about every other occupation common in a modern country.

Although more than 95 percent of the population is of Dutch extraction, there is no easy way to describe a typical Dutch person. People look and talk differently from province to province. In Friesland, the Frisian language predominates. Nearly two-thirds of the 600,000 people in Friesland speak this second language. Road signs are in both Dutch and Frisian, and many schools are bilingual.

In the north, many Dutch are tall, blue eyed, and blond. In the south, most have dark hair and eyes and slighter builds. The cities are a mosaic of many ethnic groups. These include immigrants from former colonies, including the Moluccas, Suriname, and the Netherlands Antilles and visiting workers from Turkey, Morocco, and Germany.

Holidays and Traditions

Many holidays in the Netherlands are a time of joyous celebrations, colorful costumes, and special delicacies. Others are a time for solemn prayer and silent commemoration.

Every year, children throughout the country anxiously await Sinterklaas Dag, or St. Nicholas Day. Coming about three weeks before Christmas, on December 6, St. Nicholas Day is celebrated by all religions in the Netherlands. St. Nicholas, a Catholic bishop who lived hundreds of years ago, helped to feed and clothe the poor and became known for his good deeds. Over the years, it became a

54

The figure of Sinterklaas, who delivers gifts to good children, is a familiar sight on December 6. His name is derived from St. Nicholas, a Catholic bishop known for his good deeds; this representative bears a traditional bishop's miter (hat) and crosier (staff), as well as the characteristic long, fluffy white beard.

custom for Dutch men to dress up in red-and-white bishop's robes and go from house to house bearing gifts for children. When the Dutch settled in America in the 17th century, they brought this tradition with them. American children came to pronounce Sinterklaas as Santa Claus—but clearly it was the same jolly, roly-poly man who dressed in a red suit, spreading cheer throughout the land.

Christmas in the Netherlands is celebrated on two days—December 25 and 26. Unlike St. Nicholas Day, Christmas is a solemn holiday. During the month before Christmas, farmers perform the *midwinterhoornblazen*, or Midwinter Horn Blowing. The farmers stand over their wells and blow into thin, hollow logs. The sound of the horns resonates throughout the land, announcing the coming of Christ.

On New Year's Eve, the country shuts down after 9 P.M. At midnight, ships in the harbor let loose with a symphony of horns; churches ring their melodious bells, and the sky ignites with multicolored fireworks. Passersby on the streets call out, *Zalig uiteinde*, or "Blessed end" to one another. Families gather to enjoy a hearty meal of New Year's Eve favorites, such as *oliebollen* (deep-fried dough balls studded with raisins) and *sneeuwballen* (whipped cream snowballs).

In contrast to the lively celebration of New Year's Eve, Memorial Day is a low-key, reflective holiday. On May 4, at exactly 8 P.M., all television and radio stations interrupt their usual programming. Cars and buses pull over to the side of the road. In a moment of peace, the Dutch pause to commemorate the end of World War II, to remember those killed in the war, and to pray for peace in the future. The next day is Liberation Day, when the people's cherished freedom is celebrated.

A birthday is a special day for every Dutch man, woman, and child. Most homes prominently display a calendar listing each family member's birthday. Birthdays begin when the *jarige*, or birthday person, arises. Family members come into the bedroom to presents gifts and candies and to sing a birthday song. That afternoon or evening, guests begin to file in to say *hartelijk gefeliciteerd* (happy birthday) and to present gifts. The guests are greeted with a variety of cakes, cookies, and other sweets to celebrate the festive day.

Leisure Activities

Perhaps because the Dutch are such a hardworking and disciplined people, the they make the most of their free time. And because one-sixth of the Netherlands is covered with water, the Dutch spend much of their leisure time in, on, or near the water.

The Eleven Towns Skating Race has been held fewer than 20 times this century, for the weather is not often cold enough or the ice thick enough over the length of its 120-mile (192-kilometer) course. When conditions are right, however, thousands of hardy Dutch skaters flock to the grueling marathon.

No closet in a Dutch home would be complete without several pairs of ice skates. When the weather gets very cold in the winter, people head out to the nearest frozen river, lake, or canal. It is common to see hundreds of men, women, and children ice-skating along a frozen waterway on a clear, cold day.

If the weather gets cold enough, and the ice gets thick enough, thousands of skaters participate in the Eleven Towns Skating Race.

Held in Friesland, this grueling 120-mile (192-kilometer) race winds its way through 11 adjoining towns over a series of connecting canals. Those who make it to the finish line have endured bitter cold, biting winds, ragged ice—and perhaps even fractured bones.

When the weather gets warmer and the ice disappears, people take to what many consider the number one national sport: fishing. On a warm summer day, hundreds of anglers line up along the rivers and canals. Sitting on folding chairs under big, black fishing umbrellas, the anglers reel in perch or pike from the muddy waters. On some mornings, angling clubs meet to hold contests. The prize goes to the angler who catches the longest "line" of fish laid together head to tail.

Boating is another popular pastime in the Netherlands. Whether in an old-fashioned wooden sailboat or a 50-foot flat-bottomed boat, the Dutch love to spend weekends on the water. It takes experience, however, to navigate the waterways. A skipper must avoid the barges and tankers on the rivers and canals, be wary of sandbars on the sea, and pay attention to the locks, which raise and lower the water levels in the canals and rivers.

There are about 9 million bicycles for the 14,615,000 people in the country. Bicycling is not only an important means of transportation, but also one of the most popular leisure activities. Running alongside the highways and waterways are 600 miles (966 kilometers) of bicycle paths. Bicycles are built with practicality in mind. They come complete with luggage carriers, coat and skirt protectors, mud guards, several gear speeds, and fat tires. On a warm summer day, it is not unusual to see a family of five spinning down a path, carried by only two bicycles.

Queen Beatrix was crowned in April 1980 when her mother, Juliana, who had ruled since 1948, stepped down from the throne. Beatrix earned a doctorate in sociology at the University of Leiden, married Prince Claus von Amsberg in 1966, and has three children.

6

Government and Society

Although Amsterdam is the capital of the Netherlands, the seat of national government is located in The Hague. Queen Beatrix's official residence and both chambers of parliament are there, as well as the majority of government offices.

The Netherlands operates under a form of government known as a constitutional monarchy. The king or queen, called the monarch, is the head of state. The monarch and the ministers of several national departments are together known as the Crown. Queen Beatrix Wilhelmina Armgard has been the monarch since 1980. She is a member of the royal family called the House of Orange-Nassau that is linked historically to Prince William of Orange, the Father of the Netherlands. The monarchy is inherited by the eldest male or female child of the previous monarch.

At the heart of the government lies the constitution, a set of laws that calls for basic freedoms of speech, of religion, of the press, and of association and assembly. The constitution spells out the powers of the monarch, the parliament, the judiciary, and the provincial and municipal governments. The constitution may be amended (changed) only by a bill passed by both chambers of parliament and agreed to at each stage by the king or queen.

The Crown shares legislative responsibilities with the States-General (*Staten-Generaal* in Dutch), or parliament, a body of law-makers similar to the Congress in the United States. The States-General is divided into two chambers. The first chamber consists of 75 members who are elected by representatives of each province. The second chamber has 150 members who are directly elected by the people of the Netherlands. Although both chambers may pass laws, only the second chamber has the authority to propose new laws.

In contrast to the United States, which has only two effective political parties, the Netherlands has numerous powerful political

The 225-member Dutch parliament meets in this building in The Hague. The parliament is bicameral (divided into two chambers), with 75 lawmakers in the first chamber and 150 in the second.

parties. The Christian Democratic Alliance, the Calvinist Political Union, and the People's Party for Freedom and Democracy, among others, vie to have their party members elected to the States-General. Every four years, following the general elections to the second chamber, the States-General begins a bargaining process to form a new majority government in parliament. This process is led by a *formateur*. The formateur recommends to the monarch members of parliament to be appointed ministers for justice, defense, foreign affairs, transport and public works, and education and science (different departments of the government). When this process is complete, the monarch appoints the ministers and usually names the formateur the prime minister, or head of the national government. Together, the ministers form the cabinet, which coordinates government policy.

In addition to the States-General, the Council of State and General Chamber of Audit serve as advisory and administrative bodies to the Crown. The Council of State is the highest advisory body in the Netherlands. The monarch serves as president, and the council can have as many as 28 members, who are appointed for life. Ministers seek the views of the council on all legislation being introduced. The General Chamber of Audit is responsible for managing the country's finances. The three members and their deputies keep track of the revenues and expenses of the state and submit an annual report to the Crown and the States-General. This report is also published for the public and the media.

The national budget is financed in several ways. Taxes on citizens and on corporations pay for 65 percent of the government's yearly expenditures. Other sources of revenue, such as income from the sale of natural gas, pay for an additional 15 percent of the national budget. The remaining 20 percent is financed through the sale of government bonds. The federal government spends this revenue in a variety of ways to benefit the country. The highest percentage goes toward education and science, followed by social services, the interest charge on the national debt, and defense. The national government also finances some of the costs of the provincial and municipal governments.

Provincial and local governing bodies deal with local matters. Each of the 12 provinces has its own government, called a provincial council. Every four years, residents vote for members to represent them in their respective councils. These representatives then appoint a provincial executive, who is responsible for the day-to-day administration of the province. The provincial council is not divorced from the national government, however; the Crown appoints a queen's commissioner, who works with the provincial executive to maintain law and order and to oversee the water boards within each province. Also, members of the provincial council elect representatives to the first chamber of the States-General.

Local governments in the Netherlands are called municipalities. Each town and city has its own government, consisting of a burgomaster, or mayor, appointed by the Crown, a municipal council elected by local residents, and a municipal executive committee. Together, they are responsible for maintaining their municipality.

The oldest governing body in the Netherlands is called the *waterschap* (plural, waterschappen), or water control board. There are hundreds of waterschappen throughout the country, each responsible for overseeing the polders, dikes, canals, and pumping stations in a particular area. The main responsibility of the boards is to protect the land from flooding. The most important waterschappen are those located near the major rivers, the IJsselmeer, and the North Sea.

The Judicial System, Defense, and Education

There is no such thing as trial by jury in the Netherlands. Justice is administered by judges who are appointed for life. Relatively minor crimes are tried in one of 62 subdistrict courts, called *kantongerechten*. More serious breaches of law are tried in one of 19 district courts, called *rechtbanken*. A defendant who is found guilty in a subdistrict court may lodge an appeal in a district court. Likewise, one may appeal a decision from a district court in one of five courts of appeal, called *gerechtshoven*. The highest court in the land is the supreme court, which ensures that all laws are applied uniformly.

The Netherlands maintains a national defense to protect its borders and to help preserve international peace. The country is a member of the North Atlantic Treaty Organization (NATO). Its armed services comprise more than 100,000 people in the Royal

The waterschappen, *or water control boards, are the oldest governing bodies in the Netherlands. The boards oversee the complex system of canals, pumping stations, dikes, and polders that keeps the land free from floods. Drawbridges such as this one are part of the nationwide water management system.*

Netherlands Army, Navy, and Air Force, and the Military Constabulary. The constabulary is a small military detachment responsible for various aspects of security and police work. All young men in the Netherlands are obligated to enter the armed services. However, they can choose to begin their national service at age 18, 19, or 20. The length of service ranges from 14 to 17 months, depending on the person's rank and branch of service.

The Dutch place great importance on education. Nearly one in every four people in the country is enrolled in school full-time. The ratio of teachers to students is high: In primary and secondary schools, there is 1 teacher for every 15 students. Seventeen percent of the national budget is spent on education, and the minister of education and science has the largest budget in the cabinet. Illiteracy is practically unheard of in the Netherlands.

Dutch education is provided by public and private schools, both subsidized by the state. Although many private schools are operated by Protestant or Catholic organizations, the state funds both types. These private religious schools must meet standards set by the government for courses, testing, and faculty.

Parents may enroll their children in primary school as early as age four, but attendance is not compulsory until age five. Primary education in the Netherlands lasts from age 4 to age 12. During the first two years, students learn the basic skills of reading, writing, and mathematics. Over the next six years, they learn the Dutch language, history, geography, and social studies and develop their reading, writing, and mathematics skills. Students learn English in their final year of primary school.

When Dutch students finish primary school, they enter one of three types of secondary schools, depending on their aptitude. The first type is called a general secondary school, which can last either four or five years. The second type is called a pre-university school, where students take courses for six years in preparation to attend a university. The third type, called a vocational secondary school,

(continued on page 73)

SCENES OF
THE
NETHERLANDS

Overleaf: *Near Lisse, the Netherlands, workers harvest a crop of tulips. Dutch horticulturists are world renowned for the high quality of their flowering plants.*

Hikers and a bicyclist pause to admire a typically Dutch vista—windmills lining a canal. Before electrical plants replaced them, windmills powered the pumps that drained the land and kept it free of water.

Seen from atop a dike, farms and pastures laced by canals stretch to the horizon. Much of the land in the Netherlands is below sea level, and a complex system of dikes and waterways prevents the North Sea from washing over it.

The steep roof of a thatched building rises beside a canal in the town of Franeker, in the northern part of the Netherlands. The rowboats tied up alongside show that canals are used for transportation as well as for drainage.

Diners at a busy outdoor café in Utrecht enjoy the sunshine and a view of one of the city's numerous bridges.

A shopkeeper in Amsterdam sweeps the street in front of a window crammed with blue-and-white delftware and assorted knickknacks. Although much of this merchandise is meant for tourists, many Dutch homes feature cheerful displays of delftware and colorful ceramics.

*When temperatures drop and waterways freeze over, enthusiastic
Dutch ice skaters throng the canals.*

Two young women stand before The Jewish Wedding, *by Rembrandt, in the Rijksmuseum in Amsterdam. The museum welcomes crowds of visitors from around the world, who come to admire its incomparable collection of Dutch masters and other treasures of European art.*

The swirling brushstrokes of Vincent Van Gogh (1853–90) help imbue even simple landscapes with emotional resonance. This picture, now housed in the Rijksmuseum Vincent Van Gogh in Amsterdam, is one of a series he painted near the end of his life.

The Milkmaid *is one of the most widely reproduced and well loved works of Jan Vermeer (1632–75). Most of his paintings depict interior scenes of quiet domestic activity, rendered with meticulous attention to the effects of light.*

Jan Steen (1626–79) painted many canvases filled with rowdy revelers enjoying the abundance of the Golden Age of the Netherlands. Many of his works are in the Rijksmuseum, including The Happy Family, *which depicts an exuberant, impromptu musical performance after a meal.*

Two young Dutch girls on the Isle of Marken, dressed for a festival in the traditional costume of their region, playfully wave the flag of the Netherlands. If the construction of the Markerwaard polder is deemed environmentally sound, their small island will be part of a large area of new land reclaimed from the sea.

(*continued from page 64*)
prepares students for jobs in agriculture, social services, health care, commerce, and other occupations.

There are eight universities in the Netherlands and five other schools of higher education, called *hogescholen*. The government completely finances these institutions, regardless of whether they are public or private. The oldest university is the University of Leiden, founded in 1575 by Prince William of Orange. The largest is the University of Amsterdam, founded in 1632.

Health and Social Services

The Netherlands is a country that takes care of its people. The age distribution of the population is skewed toward the young and the old. Of the 14,615,000 people, 16.8 percent are age 60 or older, and 19.2 percent are under 15. An ambitious program of social welfare ensures that young and old receive adequate income, housing, and health care. Dutch families receive family allowances from the government for each child, provided certain conditions are met. Every person receives a pension beginning at age 65, regardless of occupation. The government provides financial aid to build new homes and to improve existing ones. And the state provides health insurance to those below a certain income, as well as payments to the unemployed and the disabled. It is no wonder that the Netherlands enjoys one of the highest life-expectancy rates in the world, as well as a low infant-mortality rate; women live an average of 79.7 years, and men 73.1 years. The infant-mortality rate (or number of infants who die during their first year) is 8 per 1,000 live births.

Health care in the country is designed to provide excellent service at a reasonable price. The government subsidizes health care to a limited extent, paying for vaccination programs for children, dental services in schools, the training of health-care workers, medical research, and more. However, private medical facilities provide the bulk of health care. Many of these facilities began as religious charities, and today many hospitals still operate along Catholic or

Protestant lines. There are more than 32,000 physicians in the country, about 1 for every 452 people. Hospital beds number more than 68,000, about 1 for every 212 people. These ratios are very good, even compared to other industrialized nations. It is no surprise that, with health care taking a priority in the Netherlands, the average life expectancy for men and women has risen 44 percent since 1900.

Although the government subsidizes everything from education to health care, there is a price to pay. The Dutch are one of the most heavily taxed peoples in the world. All goods and services bought in the Netherlands are subject to a kind of national sales tax, called a value-added tax. In addition, the Dutch pay taxes on income, on personal property, on stock dividends, on real estate, and to the provincial and municipal governments.

Transportation

The Netherlands is one of the few countries where traffic on the water equals traffic on the land. Thirty percent of all goods delivered to and from the European Community pass through the Netherlands' ports. Rotterdam harbor is the loading and unloading site for many of these shipments. To make Rotterdam accessible to large oil tankers, the Dutch dug a huge trench in the floor of the North Sea that enabled supertankers carrying 200,000 tons of oil to dock in Rotterdam. There are 3,000 miles (4,828 kilometers) of inland waterways in the Netherlands, and there are more vessels on the country's rivers, lakes, and canals than anywhere in the world.

This extensive system of waterways is matched by an effective system of roadways on land. There are a total of 60,284 miles (97,233 kilometers) of roads and highways running through the Netherlands, carrying nearly 5 million cars and more than 400,000 trucks and buses.

Dutch children enjoy excellent schooling, including not only classroom instruction but also visits to the numerous cultural attractions of their nation. Here, a group of students gather around The Anatomy Lesson of Dr. Tulp, *the 1632 painting that established Rembrandt's reputation.*

Bicycles and mopeds are used for more than recreation in the Netherlands. They provide an important means of transportation for people who live close to work. More than half of the people own bicycles, and the country accommodates them with hundreds of miles of bike paths running alongside highways and waterways.

Modern, efficient public transportation is available in almost every area in the country. Every year, buses, trams, and trains carry

Bicycles and electric trams help relieve the narrow streets of Amsterdam from the automobile congestion and pollution that afflict many other modern cities.

about 1 billion passengers through cities and between municipalities. The Netherlands Railways, owned by the state, links major cities with its train network. Even small towns are not forgotten when it comes to public transportation. The government finances community bus services, staffed by volunteers, for certain areas with populations of between 1,000 and 2,000 people.

The state-owned KLM Royal Dutch Airlines is the major air carrier and transports the majority of passengers and freight in the country. NLM (Dutch Airlines), a subsidiary of KLM, specializes in flights between cities in the Netherlands and to neighboring countries. Schiphol Airport, near Amsterdam, handles the bulk of air traffic.

Freedom of opinion is paramount to the Dutch, and those opinions are expressed in 4,000 newspapers, magazines, television and radio guides, and trade journals throughout the country. The government even provides financial aid to help periodicals that are struggling to stay profitable. The country's 79 daily newspapers have a total circulation of 4,500,000.

There are 4,632,846 televisions and 4,808,728 radios in the country, approximately 1 radio and 1 television for every 3 people. Although the government has ultimate control over radio and television broadcasting, it gives responsibility for programming to private organizations. These organizations, which are mainly divided along religious or political lines, work with the Netherlands Broadcasting Association (NOS) in handling technical facilities, programming, and employees.

Shipbuilding is one of many industries in the Netherlands that are tied to the sea. The huge vessel under construction is the flagship of the Holland-America cruise-ship line. The fifth ship in the line to bear the name Rotterdam, it is 758 feet (258 meters) long and can accommodate more than 1,400 passengers and a crew of 750.

7

The Economy

The Netherlands has few natural resources of its own. At one time, the Dutch exploited the great reserves of coal found in the southern province of Limburg. But the high costs of mining and the discovery of natural gas eventually eliminated coal mining.

Natural gas is a plentiful and profitable natural resource, however. Discovered during the 1950s in the northern Netherlands and under the North Sea, natural gas now contributes between 6 and 7 percent of the gross national product of $132,920,000. The Netherlands produces more than 262.4 billion cubic feet (80 billion cubic meters) of natural gas per year. The country consumes about a quarter of that amount to power its homes and industry. It exports much of the rest to West Germany, Belgium, France, Switzerland, and Italy. There are 300 natural gas wells in the province of Groningen, making it the largest gas field in the country. Natural gas is also mined under the Wadden Zee. Nederlandse Gasunie, a company partly owned by the state, is responsible for the purchase, transport, and sale of natural gas. Its fortunes varied considerably during the 1970s and 1980s. In 1976, following on the heels of the worldwide energy crisis, Nederlandse Gasunie sold 309.9 billion cubic feet (94.5 billion cubic meters) of natural gas at home and abroad. Conservation efforts and an economic recession reduced sales to 232.2 billion cubic feet (70.8 billion cubic meters) in 1982. Sales rose again by the end of the 1980s.

Petroleum is scarce in the country. There are oil wells in the provinces of Drenthe and South Holland and under the North Sea, but they produce only 25,548,000 barrels a year. That is only 14 percent of the Netherlands' requirements. Although the Dutch do not extract much crude oil from the ground, their country is the site of one of the largest oil-refining centers in Europe. In Rotterdam, huge oil plants process and refine bulk crude oil and export the finished products to other countries.

Land in the Netherlands does not lend itself to growing high-yield crops, such as wheat and corn. For that reason, most cereals and grains the Dutch consume are imported, especially from the United States and Canada. However, one fourth of the country's land is under cultivation, producing potatoes, sugar beets, lettuce, tomatoes, cucumbers, melons, pears, cherries, grapes, apples, and strawberries.

One crop is meant not to be eaten but to be admired: tulips. Tulips and tulip bulbs are synonymous with the Netherlands. Every fall, gardeners around the world plant 4 billion Dutch bulbs to beautify their surroundings. Dutch horticulturists and farmers have developed thousands of beautiful varieties of daffodils, crocuses, hyacinths, and other bulbs that are grown and shipped worldwide. The creative cultivation of flowers both in the field and under glass (in the greenhouse) has earned the Netherlands the title of the florist for Western Europe.

More than one-third of all the land in the Netherlands is pastures and meadows. This natural environment is ideal for raising dairy cattle. Indeed, the country is famous for its dairy products, particularly cheeses. There are 5 million cows in the country that produce about 10 million tons (10.7 million metric tons) of milk. This makes the Netherlands the top milk producer in the world. Much of it goes into making distinctive Dutch cheeses, such as Edam, Gouda, and Leiden, named after Dutch towns.

The Netherlands is a highly industrialized nation. Industry accounts for about 34 percent of the national income and 84 percent

The harbor of Rotterdam is the world's busiest. Dutch exports of refined oil products, natural gas, chemicals, and milk pass through Rotterdam, as do products from other Western European nations, which ship their goods down the Rhine to the busy port on the North Sea.

of all exports. Rotterdam is the center of the oil-refining industry, where five huge corporations—British Petroleum, Chevron, Esso, Royal Dutch/Shell, and the State Oil Company of Kuwait—produce 90 million tons (99.9 million metric tons) of oil. The oil produced is shipped to smaller refineries and chemical plants in Western Europe.

The chemical industry is a major contributor to the national income. Chemical products account for 17.1 percent of manufacturing exports. Between the late 1940s and the early 1970s, the growth of chemical manufacturing outpaced every other industry in the Netherlands. Today, the country produces a wide range of chemical products, including plastics, paints, soaps, fertilizers, and disinfectants.

The fertile pastures and lush meadows of the Netherlands nourish 5 million cows. The nation's thriving herds of dairy cattle make it the number one milk producer in the world.

Petrochemical and chemical products make up a substantial portion of the cargo that is shipped from Rotterdam. This canister of liquid chemicals is destined for Great Britain.

The Netherlands is also home to important manufacturers of transportation vehicles. The Fokker Company builds airplanes that are sold to KLM Royal Dutch Airlines, the state-run airline, as well as to American and European companies. Other Dutch companies manufacture automobiles, ships, buses, trains, bicycles, and many other vehicles.

The Dutch government completely or partially owns several corporations. The Dutch State Mines is one such company, located in the South Limburg area. It includes facilities to make raw materials for plastics, paints, drugs, dyes, fertilizers, and nylon. Other companies in which the state has a controlling interest include the National Savings Bank, Royal Netherlands Blast Furnaces and Steel Works, KLM, Netherlands Railways, and Nederlands Gasunie, the distributor of natural gas.

The Netherlands is poor in natural resources—only natural gas is abundant and profitable. The Dutch make the most of this fuel. This enormous machine is a dragline that creates a ditch to hold a 42-inch (107-centimeter) diameter natural gas pipe. The dragline can dig a notch more than half a mile (1 kilometer) long and 12 feet (3.75 meters) deep in one day.

The Netherlands is a member of two important economic unions: Benelux and the European Community (EC). Benelux (the name was created from the names Belgium, the Netherlands, and Luxembourg) was formed in 1948 to increase trade among the three countries. This was achieved by eliminating import duties in each Benelux nation and by installing a common tariff for imports from other countries. The European Economic Community (EEC), modeled after the Benelux union, was formed in 1958 and eliminated similar trade barriers among several European countries. Since that time, Dutch exports to the original EEC countries have risen by 20 percent, and imports from EEC countries to the Netherlands have increased by 6 percent. In the 1980s the EEC became known simply as the European Community (EC).

The Netherlands maintains one of the highest standards of living in the world. The average size household has 2.6 people, and each household has an average income equal to U.S. $23,200. And because the government provides support for housing, health care, education, and other necessities in life, most Dutch men and women are healthy, educated, and able to afford a comfortable way of life.

Despite this high standard of living, the Netherlands has been plagued with high unemployment. In 1984, unemployment reached 17.5 percent, and in 1989 it was around 12 percent. The labor force is growing at a faster rate than many countries, yet because of automation and improved efficiency, the number of jobs has declined.

Currency

Dutch currency is measured in guilders. At the end of 1989, one U.S. dollar equaled about two Dutch guilders. Each guilder comprises 100 cents. Coins include a bronze 5-cent coin and nickel 10-cent, 25-cent, 1-guilder, and 2-guilder coins. At one time, one-cent coins were in circulation but have since been removed. The central bank, called De Nederlandse Bank, issues paper bank notes in 5-, 10-, 50-, 100-, 250-, and 1,000-guilder denominations. For the benefit of blind people, all bank notes are printed with Braille-like raised dots or triangles.

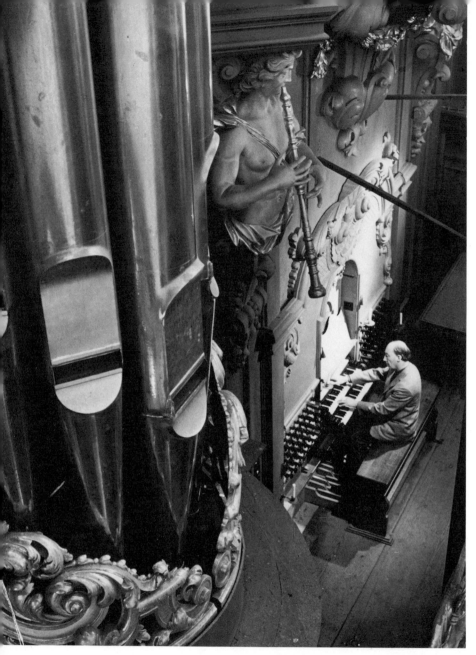

The organ of St. Bavo Cathedral in Haarlem is world renowned. Its 3 keyboards, 68 registers, and 5,000 pipes have beguiled performers and audiences alike since the days of Mozart. Here, Albert de Klerch plays the imposing instrument.

8

Culture and the Arts

The Dutch have a great love of the arts—painting, theater, dance, music, cinema, crafts, and more. This emphasis on culture is a legacy of the Golden Age in the 1600s, when Dutch artists captured Europe's imagination.

The Netherlands has been graced with an astonishing succession of brilliant painters, whose canvases have delighted millions and have found a home in the world's most prestigious museums. Artists such as Jan Van Eyck in the 15th century, Hieronymus Bosch in the 16th century, Rembrandt van Rijn in the 17th century, Vincent Van Gogh in the 19th century, and Piet Mondrian in the 20th century represent the pinnacle of achievement in the world of painting.

It is not surprising, therefore, that the Netherlands has a great number of museums and art galleries. Chief among these is the Rijksmuseum in Amsterdam, considered by scholars one of the world's greatest museums. Housed in this lavish building are more than 3,000 paintings by Jan Steen, Pieter de Hooch, Frans Hals, Jan Vermeer, Rembrandt, and others.

Another museum in Amsterdam—the Rijksmuseum Vincent Van Gogh—contains 700 paintings and drawings by this celebrated artist. His paintings of sunflowers, star-filled nights, and even his self-portrait burst with bright colors and bold, wavy paint strokes. He sold only one painting during his lifetime, but a century after his death, Van Gogh's artworks fetched tens of millions of dollars.

The Hague also boasts a world-famous museum, called the Mauritshuis. Originally built as a palace for Count Johan Maurits van Nassau in the 17th century, the Mauritshuis is now home to works by Rembrandt, Jan Vermeer, Frans Hals, and others.

Theater is popular in the Netherlands. Across the country, theater companies give about 4,500 performances a year. The government supports the dramatic arts by granting money to experimental theater companies. Unlike the repertory companies, which perform more well-known works, experimental groups try new forms of theater. For example, small groups of actors stage performances designed to make audiences more aware of social concerns, such as women's rights and family relations.

Music, like theater, is part of Dutch cultural life. The Amsterdam Concertgebouw orchestra is one of the world's great symphony orchestras. Together with the Rotterdam Philharmonic and the Residentie Orchestra of The Hague, these orchestras delight classical music lovers the world over. For classical music on a smaller scale, the Amsterdam Baroque Orchestra and the Eighteenth Century Orchestra have helped to popularize small ensembles both at home and abroad.

Wolfgang Amadeus Mozart, who as a young boy astounded Europe's royalty with his musical abilities, once performed at the St. Bavo Cathedral in Haarlem. This magnificent 16th-century structure houses the most elaborate organ in Europe. The organ boasts 3 keyboards, 68 registers, and 5,000 pipes. Organ recitals are held on Tuesdays and Thursdays throughout the summer. And since 1958, St. Bavo Cathedral has hosted the International Organ Competition, which is held every year in early July.

Dutch cinema, long hindered by the language barrier, recently has come into its own. The government-run Dutch Film Finance Corporation works together with producers, movie distributors, and theater operators to finance new films. Some of these have garnered international acclaim. The director Fons Rademakers received an Academy Award nomination for his 1958 film, *Doctor in the Village*. Nearly 30 years later, in 1987, Rademakers took home an Oscar for his film *The Assault*.

Crafts have a special place in Dutch culture. Earthenware pottery, colorful tiles, pewter mugs, willow baskets, and pendulum clocks brighten up Dutch homes and lure shoppers around the world. One particular kind of pottery, called delftware, is especially famous. Produced in the town of Delft, these vases, bowls, and plates feature delicate blue designs on a white background. Dutch seafarers brought back many of these designs from their travels in the Far East and Indonesia. Only two firms still produce delftware in the traditional way. The Royal Delft Earthenware

The Rijksmuseum in Amsterdam numbers among the world's greatest museums. Its holdings of more than 3,000 paintings, especially those of Hals, Rembrandt, and Vermeer, all masters from the Golden Age, attract scholars and art lovers from around the world.

Factory and the Royal Tichelaar Earthenware Factory use old-fashioned methods—pottery wheels, kilns, powdered charcoal stencils, and paintbrushes made from the hairs of a cow's inner ear—to produce their elegant wares.

The cultural life of the Netherlands is reflected in its distinctive cities. Four cities in particular—Amsterdam, The Hague, Rotterdam, and Utrecht—have unique personalities.

Perhaps the most well known of all Dutch cities is Amsterdam, the capital of the Netherlands. It is located at the mouth of an inland arm of the IJsselmeer and divided into two sections by the Amstel River. At one time, Amsterdam was called Amstel Dam after a wooden dam around which the original town was built. Today, this city of 679,140 retains its old-world charm. Amsterdam's historic

Amsterdam is a hotbed of liberal and revolutionary political activism. Enraged by persistent unemployment and the high cost of living space, this group of squatters, called Kabouters, took over, renovated, and occupied an abandoned building. The sign proclaims, on behalf of the house: I am not ashamed anymore, I am lived in.

homes, tree-lined canals, magnificent churches, and 550 bridges make it one of the most beautiful cities in the world.

The Dutch reputation for tolerance of all peoples and ways of life finds full flower in Amsterdam. In fact, the permissiveness in Amsterdam raises many an eyebrow in other parts of the world. Prostitution and sex boutiques are permitted in certain zones. At some cafés, customers can purchase marijuana in several varieties. In fact, prices of marijuana were actually announced over the radio at one time, but that practice has ended.

At times, this permissiveness has led to problems. In recent years, unemployed and homeless young people have illegally moved into abandoned apartments in Amsterdam. Some of these "squatters" have resorted to violence in their call for a political and social revolution, staging riots and intimidating police. But the government has sought to deal with the situation peacefully. It is not unusual to see a squatter arguing his or her point passionately with a police officer, and the officer listening more patiently than might be expected. Recently, the government has passed tougher property laws, aimed at reducing the number of squatters.

The Hague is the center of the national government. The queen's official residence when she visits The Hague is Huis ten Bosch Palace, and the city is the site of many government buildings, including the Ridderzaal (Knight's Hall), where both houses of parliament meet. The Ridderzaal, with its massive beams, stained-glass windows, and towers, was built in 1280.

The Hague is sometimes called Peace City. The first international peace conference was held in The Hague in 1899; another was held there in 1907. The American millionaire Andrew Carnegie gave $1.5 million in 1903 to build the Peace Palace, home of the Permanent Court of Arbitration, a forerunner of what is today the United Nations International Court of Justice, which is now housed there.

This city that is so closely identified with early attempts to achieve international peace was severely damaged by war. In World War II

The elegant spires of the Dom Cathedral rise gracefully at the end of a narrow cobblestone street in Utrecht.

the Germans destroyed entire parts of the city in order to build coastal defenses. One district of the city, the Bezuidenhout, was completely leveled by British bombardment. After the war the Dutch engaged in an intensive effort to rebuild and repair the war damage. In the late 20th century, The Hague is known for its quiet residential areas, numerous government offices, and the Netherlands Congress Center, one of the largest convention centers in the world.

Rotterdam is a city resurrected from ashes. The city was heavily bombed in World War II. On May 14, 1940, German bombers destroyed 35,000 buildings and devastated the country's most important seaport. Since that time, the Dutch have rebuilt Rotterdam into a modern city, glistening with new office buildings, wider streets, and an enlarged port. Today, Rotterdam is the largest seaport in the world. Its strategic location near the Rhine and Maas rivers and its access to the North Sea make it the port of choice for companies shipping goods into and out of Europe.

There is a saying, "Shirts in Rotterdam are sold with the sleeves already rolled up." With its bustling harbor, massive shipbuilding works, oil refineries, and chemical-manufacturing plants, the city is known more for its work than its play. Nevertheless, Rotterdam does have its leisure attractions. The Blijdorp Zoo in the northern part of the city is home to wild animals from around the world. The Lijnbaan shopping center is a complex of 40 shops surrounded by wide sidewalks, where only pedestrian traffic is allowed. And the Museum de Dubbelde Palmboom gives visitors a glimpse of Rotterdam's fascinating history.

Utrecht is a curious blend of historic and modern elements. Massive, historic cathedrals located near modern hotels give Utrecht a flavor all its own.

Because of its many churches, canals, and bridges, Utrecht is called the City of Spires and Bridges. The Dom Cathedral is perhaps its most famous church. It was built on the site of St. Martin's Cathedral, which was gutted by fire in the 13th century. Today, the cathedral boasts several chapels, 13 church bells, exquisite stained-glass windows, and a tower that can be reached by climbing 465 steps.

Utrecht has a special place in the hearts of the Dutch. It was here that the Union of Utrecht was formed in 1579 by the seven provinces that had united to abolish Spanish rule of the Netherlands. The urge for national freedom found its voice in the City of Spires and Bridges.

Along the canal banks of the Netherlands, stolid fishermen in folding chairs, accompanied by a patient cat, await the nibble of a pike. The recent efforts of the Dutch to clean up their environment are an attempt to preserve their land and waters for the enjoyment of future generations.

9

The Future of the Netherlands

In the course of their colorful history, the Dutch have won many battles. They have fought off foreign rulers through daring and determination. They have wrested land from the sea and turned it into productive farmland and thriving cities. The works of their great artists and thinkers have touched people around the earth. Their standard of living is one of the highest in the world. By their efforts they have demonstrated that a country's greatness need not be limited by its size.

But progress has brought problems as well. The country's dense population and the spectacular growth of Dutch industry have contributed to pollution of the air, water, and land. Today, the Netherlands is one of the world's most polluted countries. However, as the Dutch have demonstrated so often in the past, few problems are unsolvable. With their characteristic creativity, tenacity, and emphasis on organization, they have devised a solution that matches the scale of the Delta Project.

In 1989, the government proposed one of the most massive environmental programs ever conceived by one country. The

The Summit on the Protection of the Global Atmosphere held at the Peace Palace in The Hague in 1989 attracted numerous protesters who supported multinational attempts to prevent air pollution. Their signs bore slogans in Dutch, English, and a multitude of other languages.

Netherlands is resolved to eliminate 70 percent of its pollution by the year 2010. By 1994, the government plans to double its spending for environmental efforts to $8.2 billion a year. The new measures will affect every segment of the population, not only industry. By greatly reducing air, water, and soil pollution, by decreasing energy consumption and the volume of wastes, and by increasing the use of public transportation, the government intends to clean up the environment in 20 years.

The population density of the Randstad remains a problem. Nearly half of the Dutch population—6 million people—lives in this urban ring in the western part of the country. The Randstad includes several major cities, including Amsterdam, Rotterdam, Utrecht, and Leiden. These and other towns are separated from each other by strips of more or less open area that are together called the Green Heart. However, as the major cities spread closer to each other, and as more and more suburbs are built in the Green Heart, this land is becoming less and less open. In fact, the Green Heart now has the same population density as the national average.

The government has responded with a plan called concentrated deconcentration. To accommodate growth, it has designated a

The startlingly modern architecture of this building is typical of the innovative Dutch approach to housing and serving a large population concentrated in a small area. The inhabitants of the Netherlands continue to lead the way in finding efficient and interesting solutions to contemporary problems.

limited number of growth towns in or near the Randstad. By restraining expansion elsewhere and targeting these growth towns, the Dutch hope to ease the population density in the major cities, confine the spread of suburbs, and keep the Green Heart as green as possible.

Despite its problems, the Netherlands remains a triumphant example of good planning. Its streets are clean. Its people are healthy. Its economy is fit. Its government is stable. The Netherlands is a nation shaped by the perseverance and fortitude of its people. They have experienced a struggle against nature that is unique in the history of mankind. Centuries of fighting back the rising tides have instilled a sense of organization and of community among the Dutch. One Dutch saying, *Ik roei met de riemen die ik heb,* can be roughly translated, "I'll make the best of the situation." But the Dutch have done more than just make the best of it. A visitor to the Netherlands sees Holstein cows grazing on land that was once underwater, a city rebuilt from rubble, and dikes, dams, canals, and bridges built by people determined to create a home in an inhospitable environment. The Dutch continue to impress the world with their drive and accomplishments.

The Netherlands is best summed up by a quote from a travel book written more than 100 years ago: "The Dutch made it; it exists because the Dutch preserve it; it shall vanish whenever the Dutch shall abandon it."

GLOSSARY

Benelux An economic union formed by Belgium, the Netherlands, and Luxembourg in 1948 to increase trade among the three countries.

Boers A group of Dutch farmers who settled in South Africa during the 1600s.

Delftware Produced in the town of Delft, these vases, bowls, and plates feature delicate blue designs on a white background.

Erwtensoep A thick pea soup often served at the beginning of dinner.

Gerechtshoven A court where one may appeal a decision from a district court.

Gezellig A Dutch word to describe the feeling of coziness, comfort, and pleasure.

Groentensoep A clear broth filled with miniature meatballs, vegetables, and noodles.

Grote schoonmaak The "spring cleaning" conducted by most households for two or three weeks every year.

Guilder The basic unit of Dutch currency, which is divided into 100 cents.

"Hartelijk gefeliciteerd"	A Dutch phrase meaning "happy birthday."
Jarige	A Dutch man, woman, or child celebrating a birthday.
Kantongerechten	A lower court where relatively minor crimes are tried.
Klompen	Wooden shoes worn by people who work outdoors, such as fishermen, farmers, and gardeners.
Kopje koffie	A cup of coffee at midmorning.
Marram	A type of grass planted on the coastal dunes to protect them from the ravages of wind.
Midwinterhoornblazen	The Midwinter Horn Blowing. A Christmas tradition in which farmers stand over their wells and blow into thin, hollow logs to announce the coming of Christ.
Oliebollen	Deep-fried dough balls studded with raisins. A favorite treat served on New Year's Eve.
Polder	An area of land that has been separated from the sea by dikes and drained of water.
Rechtbanken	A district court where more serious breaches of the law are tried.
Sneeuwballen	Whipped cream snowballs served on New Year's Eve.
Terps	Man-made islands, constructed by the Frisians 2,500 years ago. These huge mounds of earth and clay were a crude yet effective attempt to stave off the North Sea.
Waterschap	A water control board responsible for overseeing the polders, dikes, canals, and pumping stations in a particular area.
"Zalig uiteinde"	A common Dutch expression, meaning "Blessed end," that is exchanged on New Year's Eve.

INDEX

101